ONLY IN MY DREAMS

DAWN COLCLASURE

EDITED BY
KEVIN SAITTA

This book is dedicated to every person in my life who has loved, accepted, and embraced both the old and new me, as well as the new people who love, accept, and support the new me. I love you all!

DREAM POEMS

INTRODUCTION

Poetry has held an important role in my life from a very young age, especially during my recovery from an auto accident that inflicted me with third-degree burns. Dreams, too, have played a big part in shaping my existence. In my early childhood, some had a precognitive quality. As a lonely teenager striving to find love in the real world, they provided a source of affection and romance. For a burn survivor rejected by society, they became my refuge. And as a Deaf individual, they offered me solace that I couldn't experience in waking life.

At the age of sixteen, a recurring dream experience set me on a lifelong path of researching, studying, and interpreting dreams. Indeed, dreams hold a prominent place within my family, often serving as topics of discussion and analysis. Their influence on my writing has been profound, leading me to create a poetry chapbook titled "Dream World," dedicated to exploring the realm of dreams.

I am excited to unite these two passions in a poetry collection comprising forty-nine poems that dive into these themes and the many enigmas surrounding them. The title of the collection itself reflects on how certain experiences, like reuniting with lost loved ones or rectifying disabilities, can only be attained in the realm of our sleep. My aspiration is to convey a message of hope, inspiration, and a deeper appreciation for the power of dreams through the publication of this book.

I

NO LIMITS IN MY DREAMS

I can't hear in the real world,
but I hear everything in my dreams.
There's no such thing as deafness
or blindness, as everyone can see.

I seldom see anyone in a wheelchair
or anyone who requires help to walk.
Everyone has the ability to do everything,
including things not possible when awake in life.

The dream world is an escape from reality,
a place where everyone is free.
Not just free of disabilities
but free of the responsibilities holding us down deep.

Of course, there are nightmares
to remind us of the bad and good in between.
But in dreams, we are free of worldly restrictions,
And of diseases that end our lives incomplete.

2

ONLY IN MY DREAMS

How can this be?
He's just a dream
and, yet, I feel his love.

How can this be?
He isn't a real person,
but he's all I can think of.

How can this be?
My heart yearns for him
yet he is only in my dreams.

How can this be?
This is just a dream of love
but it's more real than love seems.

3
DREAM VISITS

You've been gone for years,
yet sometimes I see you in my dreams.
You are my mother, my father, my grandmother, or
    even my aunt,
who is paying me a visit once again.

Sometimes, we share happy stories
or sit with our cups of coffee to talk.
We work on things together
and visit the others who miss you too.

I wish these dreams were real-world visits,
even if only for a brief stay.
I miss hugging you and spending time with you.
I miss seeing your smile and creating memories
    with you.

You can't come back to life in the real world,
but at least you're alive when you visit in my dreams.
Somehow, these visits make it easier to go on without
    you,
until that day comes when we'll always be together
    again.

4

JUST A DREAM?

"It's just a dream," they all say
but is that even true?
Some dreams may not make sense
but some try to teach something new.

And sometimes, in the dreams we have,
we are forced to face a fear,
or try to sort through our worries
when no other help is near.

In some dreams, we see loved ones long gone,
or hear their distant voices.
In other dreams, we try to understand
how to make our choices.

Not all dreams are meant to be anything,
but some dreams might bring us pause.
These are the dreams we should pay attention to,
because they are the dreams with a cause.

5

NIGHTMARES

I know they're just a dream.
I know they're not real.
But they're so scary and horrific,
a very real terror that I feel.

The fear a nightmare brings to me
grips me so deeply within my soul.
Deep inside, my heart freezes with terror.
The horrors take their toll.

It doesn't help knowing my imagination
can come up with such an atrocity.
I'm all alone when I face these horrors,
no one is there for me.

All my fears and all my worries,
they haunt me when I sleep.
I try to think of other things,
but the horror touches me so deep.

6

DREAMS THAT LINGER

Some dreams are so real and strong,
they can't be tossed away.
They are dreams that stay within
our memories every day.

They can be dreams of a lost loved one
or snippets from a song.
We can remember them as if they're real
and those memories stay so long.

It could be a dream about our friends,
or a warning of danger.
A dream in which we lost control
and gave into our hate and anger.

I think about such dreams to try and understand —
will this make them disappear?
For now, we can only remember and talk to
    comprehend
while these dreams continue to linger here.

7
LIVING LIVES

First, I am a firefighter,
putting out the flames.
Second, I am a teacher
reading a list of my student's names.

Then, I am a character
in a TV show which I enjoy.
In the next, I am a homeless mother
giving birth to a baby boy.

Or perhaps I live in a game,
one that I like to play on the computer.
Maybe I am some disgruntled student,
angry at my tutor.

Sometimes, I'll be a bug, a bird, a flying squirrel,
or a ghost that makes people scream.
Eventually, I'll wake up and be me again,
because it was all just another dream.

8

DREAM LOVER

The love in my dreams that I share with you,
it's a strong love that never ends.
But it's a love that no one understands.
"Forget it," says family and friends.

How can I forget your face,
or our love, so strong?
I cannot push these dreams from me.
I don't think that they are wrong.

They are only dreams, I know.
Dreams of love and passion, so true.
Dream lover, never leave my dreams.
May I always dream of you.

I've never known a love like this.
No one in real life loves me like you do.
Dream lover, never leave my dreams.
May I always dream of you.

9

WHEN I DREAM OF YOU

When I dream of you,
you are my dream come true.
No matter where you are,
whether you're near or far.

The bright light shining in your eyes
is like the morning's breathtaking sunrise.
Your sweet smile and soft touch,
These dreams of you mean so much.

Every night, I wish to see you
in my dreams right here with me.
And when I sleep to find you there,
it's a dream come true for us to share.

I never want to see you go,
my dreams of you are all I know.
They are just for us to be together.
I want to dream of you forever.

10

ADVENTURES IN DREAMING

Tonight, I will embark on a new adventure.
Tonight, I will dream.
My dreams tell me what none other could,
what a lifetime of studying could never gleam.

When I dream, I know my heart.
I know who I really am.
What I would never, ever do,
why I even give a damn.

My dreams present new challenges.
They test all that, I believe.
They ask me what I would sacrifice
and for whom I'd grieve.

My dreams help me find closure,
they answer "what if?" to see what I would do.
I look forward to each night that I dream
to see what more I will find new.

II

REGRET

I should've kept it in my dreams,
why did I try to make it real?
It doesn't matter who that was,
or how the dreams made me feel.

I should've kept it in my dreams,
they were something only in my mind.
It was not something I could create in life,
or something I could find.

I should've kept it in my dreams,
it was just a dream, after all.
It didn't guide my path in life
or give me a divine call.

It was just a dream and nothing more,
wherein it should have stayed.
I now know the pain of trying to make a dream come
     true,
and the price that I have paid.

12

DREAM MAN

First, I see him in my dreams,
and I think he's only a dream.
And then I tell someone I know;
she smiles as her eyes begin to gleam.

The man in my dreams is much the same,
as a man that the world knows —
Same name, same face, and the same eyes.
He's loved everywhere he goes.

My heart falls into confusion and angst,
because it's the man in my dreams I love.
Yet, a man has his face and name in the real world,
but he's not a man I know of.

My heart only focuses on my dream man,
because it's in my dreams where my heart is won.
The real man is not the man in my dreams;
my heart says my dream man is the one.

13

IN MY MIND

Questions linger in my mind,
the things I will not write or say.
Then he comes to me in dreams
to explain them away.

He presents people in my dreams as I know them,
then shows me the true face that they hide.
He is not just someone in my dreams who I love;
he is also some kind of a guide.

Can I believe the things he says?
There is some possibility with what he shows,
he makes me wonder what else in my mind he reads
and what other things he knows.

My mind's no longer a solitary place
to ponder things and indulge in fantasy.
It's as though my dream man knows what's in
    my mind
and uses my dreams to share what he knows with me.

14
WORLDS APART

Our love is stronger than any kind
of love we have felt before.
If only we could be together.
If only we could have more.

But our lives cannot be shared as one,
as they were right from the start.
We are forced to live between two worlds.
Living each day in worlds apart.

At night, my dreams bring us together,
even if it couldn't be real.
But in my dreams, the love we have for one another
is something strong we feel.

One day we shall be reunited,
and until then, you have my heart.
I can only see your face,
you could only hear my voice,
as we live in worlds apart.

15

MY OWN DREAM MAN

What are these dreams that I keep having,
What do they really mean?

This older man in my dreams
wants something from me.
I don't understand; I'm only sixteen.

The dreams continue, anyway.
Who is this man I see?

I have his name and image therein,
He's all I seem to see.

I tell one sister about my dreams,
and there's something that makes her feel,
that the man in my dreams portrays a man
who might be very real.

I see a picture in real life
and I'm surprised at what I see.
The man in the photo looks the same
as the man in the dreams;

The same face,
The same first name,
I can't help but wonder – could it be?

But in my dreams, I'm told no —
It's something else I should know.

Clues are given,
As time passes on,
Then, finally, the mystery unfolds.

My love was real for this man in my dreams,
My heart never went cold.
Years later, he still visits me;
In my dreams, I can finally see.

16

DREAM SOUNDS

I hear your voice in my dreams.
Is this how you sound?
When I hear a phone ring in my dreams,
it's not a noise that's found.

I cannot hear in my waking life,
but when I dream, my hearing is there.
I hear somebody's voice or an old song,
The creaking screech of a rocking chair.

The barking sound of a distant dog,
Music playing from a source I cannot see.
A baby's cry, a toy's squeak,
The splashing waves while at sea.

I wonder if all these sounds are true,
If, at least, that's how people sound.
I can't hear at all in my waking life,
but in my dreams, noise is all around.

17
WHAT ARE DREAMS?

What are dreams?
Are they an escape?
Are they some fantasy world
for us to escape?

Are dreams a warning?
A visitation from the dead?
Are dreams meant to entertain
in their own bizarre ways?

How do we make dreams?
Will the dreams we have ever be real?
Is there really such a thing as a dream come true?
For now, dreams are our only way to be free.

18

DREAM COME TRUE

My dream was so amazing.
If only it could be real!
It made me feel so excited.
It is something I again want to feel.

I want what happened in my dream
to become a reality.
It really was an awesome thing
and it meant so much to me.

I will try to make my dream come true
in any way that I can.
That thing is something I really want.
And so, I'll make a plan.

I'll do what I can to make my dream come true,
so that it can be a part of my real life.
I'll do what it takes to make that happen,
no matter the troubles or the strife.

19

SUCH DREAMS

There are no dreams as profound
as the ones that touch the soul.
The ones that make us do something,
to spring into action.

Such dreams are like a gift from the universe,
a little nudge in a certain direction.
They have that kind of effect on us,
that this is something we must know or do.

Or sometimes a dream will provide us with answers
to things we struggle to understand when awake.
Answers so clear and solutions so perfect,
and we know right away that they are the right ones.

Then there are such dreams we may have
when a loved one is there for a visit.
They may look different or they may look the same.
Seeing them again in our dreams appeases our soul
    and gives comfort.

20

INTERRUPTED BLISS

I wish I didn't wake from my dream.
I was so happy there!
Especially being with people I love
and for those whom I really care.

Just being in my dream with him brought me peace
and a sense of happiness that is hard to find.
The love he shows me in my dreams
is always the most tender and kind.

Not to say that I am not happy here,
in the life that I share with people I hold dear.
I enjoy the people who surround my days
and the tasks I perform that make my path clear.

But the dreams I have with loved ones and my own
    dream man
happen so very rarely, they are dreams I don't wish
    to end.
Awakening from these dreams when they rarely do
    occur
causes a pain in my heart that takes ages to mend.

21

CREATING MY OWN DREAMS

If I could create my own dreams,
there would never be any nightmares.
No monsters hiding under my bed.
No angry school teacher shaking a ruler at me.

My dreams would be filled with everyone I love
and everyone in my life I call friend.

My dreams would be wild adventures
and filled with creatures where we could talk.

My dreams would be set in such beautiful worlds,
full of fantasy, magic, and wonder.
With interesting sights to see wherever I go
and fun things to do, like slide down a rainbow.

If only I could create my own dreams
and enjoy such fantasies while I sleep.

What wonderful dreams would be had,
and each dream would last forever.

22

ANIMALS AND DREAMS

Do animals dream?
Sometimes, I think so.
Watching a dog sleeping
and his legs moving
as though he is running
through a field of some sort.

Watching cats react in their sleep,
a sudden reaction
to something only they can see.
Probably watching other cats at play
or just knocking something off the table.

If animals do dream,
what kind of dreams do they have?
Are they always themselves in a dream?
Are they ever a human?

I wonder what
an animal's dream would be like
if they were a different species.

Would they be able to create a better world?

23
A CALL TO ACTION

Last night, I dreamed
that I rescued some rats
from being gassed to death.
This is something I'd do
in real life, if in such a situation.
But the people killing the rats
thought it was more humane
to gas them to death
instead of using traps.

This reminds me of the pigs,
gassed to death before slaughter.
Some believe it's more humane,
But they have no idea
the kind of suffering a pig will endure.

Humans suffered when being gassed,
during the time of Hitler's power.

There's nothing humane
about ending a life
through a gassing chamber.

But what else is this dream telling,
To allow me to see?

One of the rats that looked like a pig.
Am I being called to action?

I have spoken out about such carnage.
What more must I do?

24

DREAM KARMA

Is there such a thing as dream karma?

Do actions in dreams
overlap into real life,
creating some kind of good vibe?

Perhaps good deeds in our dreams
may inspire us to do good when awake.

Then, we can attract good karma,
all thanks to our dream.

25
WHAT DOES IT MEAN?

What does it mean
when we fly in our dreams?
Or when we plant a certain flower?
Or find a strange coin?

We all have ideas
about symbolism in our dreams.
Most of it is based on what experts of the past
had to say about this or that.

But, we now know better;
More research has been done —
The subject has been debated,
Some old beliefs are replaced with new ones.

But maybe it all comes down
To the person who had the dream.
Their own interpretation is based on what they see.
Sometimes, a flower is just a flower.

26

MY DREAMS OF YOU

My dreams of you
do my heart good
To see you smiling again.
To hear the sound of your laugh.

Hugging you is not the same
as it would be in real life,
but hugging you in my dream
is still just as good because it's you.

You, who has been gone for so long.
You, who I miss every day.
When I dream of you, these visits, though brief,
help chase my tears away.

My dreams of you are so brief
and there's so much more I wish to say.
But I am still grateful to see you again
and to spend time with you in some way.

27

MIXED MESSAGES

I wonder if I got the right message
from the dream that I had.

Did I do what the dream said I should?

Did I interpret the symbolism correctly?

I spent some time trying to figure it out,
I knew it was more than a dream.

This dream had a message for me,
A hidden meaning for me to see.

28
DREAMS ARE...

Dreams are
a sleep-induced escape,
where we visit other worlds.

Dreams are
a chance to explore other realities
which we humans may never know.

Dreams are
other lives in alternate universes,
where we live as our twin or someone else.

Dreams are
modes of time travel,
where we live in the past or the future.

29

DISCOVERING THE SECRETS

People hide things from us all the time.
The truth about things,
how much money they really spent
or their true feelings,

And they believe this works;
that no one but them
will ever know
any of these secrets.

But think again.
There are some people
gifted with the ability
to uncover these secrets in their dreams.

There are no secrets.
There never can be.
Our loved ones on the other side know all
and they will share those secrets with us in our
　　dreams.

30
TRANSLATING OUR DAYS

They say that when we dream,
our brain is still hard at work.
Sifting and sorting,
analyzing and exploring.

Our brains are like a tape recorder
that runs during our day.
And then, at night, when we sleep,
our brains replay the tape, going over our whole day.

The claim is that when our brains
replay our days,
they influence our dreams
we have that night.

Somehow, things get lost in translation.
The images are deciphered all wrong.
We may have multiple dreams and none of them
would have anything to do with the recording our
    brain plays.

31

A SOURCE OF INSPIRATION

Can our dreams inspire us to change?
To find the strength to try?
Can they help us find the confidence
to look someone in the eye?

Can our dreams inspire good actions?
Can they make us a better person?
Can our dreams provide the answer to conflict
before they continue to worsen?

We don't give much credit to our dreams
Because, most of the time, they don't make sense.
But dreams can hold the key to our deepest desires
and help us see things through a better lens.

Throughout history, dreams have guided people
and inspired them to do more.
Dreams have the power to help us understand the
    things
in ways we hadn't thought to understand them
    before.

32
UNRESOLVED ISSUES

The things we bury inside of ourselves
can manifest in our dreams.
No matter how we wish to forget,
they play out as our nightmares or dreams.

For years, I struggled with nightmares
of abuse, being manipulated and used.
Those things from my past hurt me still,
and they hurt even worse when I sleep.

I think it helps to get some counseling,
but we are the ones who need to heal.
We need to overcome the pain and find peace,
or those dreams will only continue to haunt us.

Everything that we try to avoid from the past
has a way of appearing in our dreams.
We can choose to allow it to be a thorn in our sides
or find some way to let go and move on.

33
FINDING ANSWERS IN DREAMS

I could not figure out a thing,
so at day's end, I stopped trying.
I decided that today wouldn't be the day
to find the solution I required.

Instead, I went to bed,
I'll try again tomorrow.
But as I lie, I still contemplated.
It's hard for me to let go.

Then, I gradually drifted off to sleep,
only to dream of the solution I seek.
And in the morning, after I woke,
I could've forgotten, but thankfully, I took note.

I wrote down the solution that transpired,
thankful for the answer the dream inspired.
Sometimes, my dreams help me understand things a
    little better,
or provide a solution for that which is dire.

34

DREAM ME

"Dream Me" does some crazy things!
Things in real life I would never do.
Like flush my kid's clothes down a toilet,
be around toxic people, or fake having the flu.

"Dream Me" takes some patience to interpret her
    reasons
and a little time to get used to and understand.
I am certainly not like the me in my dreams,
who hurts so easily and takes things out of hand.

But the me that I am in my dreams
is one I like to study, because she is so surprising.
Her lives are unlike mine and she is more attractive.
I never tire of the different "Dream Me" these dreams
    bring.

Is Dream Me better than the real me that I am?
She has qualities and looks which I adore.
But I'm grateful that I am not really her.
When these dreams end, I'm glad I'm not Dream Me
    anymore.

35
THE MESSAGE

I had a dream that provided a message,
but I'm not sure it's something I should heed.
The message contains things about me,
something I'm going through that I must flee.

But what if the dream was just a dream,
and not something more?
What if the person was just saying
the thing my subconscious KNOWS I need.

If I say I received the message from the middle of my
     sleep,
people will be skeptical, and others won't believe.
Many accept reality but not the message from a
     dream.
So, I can't use the message for my needs.

Yes, people in the past have turned to dreams,
especially when struggling with earthly deeds.
But can I rely on the message in my dream?
Or might it end up only making things worse than
     reality?

36

HAPPY DREAMS

What a wonderful thing to have a happy dream,
one that's filled with joy.
The kind of dream I have always hoped for,
the kind that erases my sadness and pain.

A happy dream that creates a lingering sense of joy
    after I awaken,
one that is safe to experience and allow to linger for a
    long time.
It is the kind where I want this sense of euphoria to
    never end.
I will remember it when I want or need to feel cheerful
    again.

37

THE BAD ENDING

When I wake from a dream that has a bad ending,
or something that happens that could make me cry,
I try to rewrite that terrible ending
so that it's not something that would make me sigh.

Instead of a dog falling from way up in the sky,
a hero catches him so that he will live.
The animal my sibling tortured is rushed to the
    hospital.
There is so much relief these better endings can give.

The car I'm driving that goes off of a cliff
lands on a bridge that will suddenly appear.
The child who is being beaten by a parent
is rescued and no longer must live in fear.

Some endings I make up may not be realistic
but at least they take away the sadness and anger.
I pretend these new endings are how the dream really
    ended
because it's easier to believe that there is no more
    danger.

38
WHAT IF?

Dreams are a chance for us to explore
so many possibilities we can't ignore.
Our creativity thrives when we sleep,
making them more exciting and deep.

What if we had a woman for a President?
A dream can show what life would be like.
What if dogs could talk?
What interesting conversations that would shock!

What if the sky was a different color
with three Suns in the middle of summer?
Our dreams could shed light on such a world
and give us a taste of something to adore.

Our dreams allow us to explore the "what if's?"
Answer to help ideas that can shift.
What kind of place would our world be,
if we tried to make all those things a true reality?

39

THE SAME DREAM

What does it mean
when we have the same dream?
I'd like to know,
as it's an unusual thing.

Are we supposed to do something else?
Is there a meaning we all need to see?
Does this predict something bad or obscene?
Should we change plans that we all seek?

When we all have the same dream,
that's when we all know
perhaps it was not "just a dream"
and there is more there we must see.

It's possible the subconscious fed off a common
    feeling
and caused us all to have the same dream at one time.
It's very hard to understand how this could happen,
and it can be even harder to understand what it
    means.

40
OBSESSION

I can't help obsessing over this!
The thing that I dream of at night.
My dreams are exactly my hopes and desires,
they strengthen my will, my obsession, my earthly
    acquires!

These are the things I can think about,
all that my dream can bring about.
Yes, I'm obsessed! These dreams are my proof
that even in sleep, I'll shout it from the roof!

41

A MESSY DREAM

Nothing in this dream makes sense!
It's such a messy dream.
It's filled with people I don't know,
suggesting a questionable scheme.

Lots of weird things are happening
and many things in this dream are not very logical.
Many things that happen are silly and impossible
and their order is not even chronological.

I guess this kind of dream is not of importance.
It's the kind of dream where anything goes.
I'd be wasting my time trying to understand the what
    and the why
because the things in this dream are stuff that nobody
    knows.

There are no rules or laws of science in dreams
and things people say can be nonsensical.
If I can't make any sense out of these messy dreams,
then maybe I could use some interpretation to wax
    philosophical.

42

CONNECTION REQUEST

I get connection requests through social media,
but is it possible to get them in our dreams as well?
I wonder why after having just such a dream,
but it is pretty hard for me to tell.

I haven't spoken to this person in years;
our conversation was strictly for something I was
    writing.
Is my dream telling me to reach out to check in
    with him?
It's the message this kind of dream is inciting.

I no longer write for that paper
and I have no other connection with this man.
I don't otherwise know anything else about him or his
    work.
I feel like I need to make some kind of a plan.

I feel like I should try to connect
or to send an email saying hi.
Maybe my subconscious knows something I don't.
It wouldn't hurt to at least give it a try.

43

A WASTE OF TIME?

My dream warned me that I was wasting my time
with a certain thing I have been doing.
But I thought it was the right thing to do.
Now, this dream has changed my view.

I thought that all this time,
I was doing something good.
It was a fun activity!
It put me in a happy mood.

I know it's not something I can monetize.
It's just a hobby that makes me feel vitalized.
Why would my dream tell me to stop,
and take that away to make me feel lost?

I know I shouldn't consider it much;
I HAD hoped it would help me advance to the next
     spot.
This dream warned me that it was not what I had
     hoped,
and the message within is clear and well thought.

44

THE BAD THING

Why did I have that dream?
Was it some kind of test?
I would never do such a thing!
That dream filled me with disgust.

Seeing myself do that very thing
that I said I would never do
filled me with anger when I saw myself
actually do that thing, and want to!

I know it was just a dream,
but it feels like I betrayed myself.
I went against everything I fought so hard to achieve
and throwing away this new person I became.

I gave in to temptation in my dream;
I started drinking again, but privately.
I hated seeing myself return to that life
and throw away my commitment to sobriety.

That I gave into alcoholism in secret is worse;
I knew in this dream that it was wrong.
If anything, this dream may be my reason
to keep my resolve to stay sober strong.

45

YOU CAN'T FORCE A DREAM

You can't force things with a dream,
like seeing someone or something.
You can't plan to have the kind you want
or expect them to occur any time you desire.

Dreams happen in their own way.
There is no way to control them.
We may try to make ourselves act in certain ways
but we have no way of knowing the events that take
place.

We may try to wish and hope for the kind we'd like
to have
but it usually does not mean they will unfold.
Maybe it's better that they happen in their own time,
because then we can appreciate them all the more.

The dreams we have can be so random
and there's no telling which kind will happen next.
Sometimes we know a recurrent dream will happen
    again,
but in most cases, we can't really know what to
    expect.

46

DREAM MESSAGE

Can we believe what is in a dream?
Should we follow through?
Should we do what a dream suggests?
Is what my dream's telling me true?

I often get a feeling about a dream
that perhaps it was some kind of vision.
Or some kind of message sent to me
to influence a decision.

Perhaps it's something I can just think about,
something that I can meditate upon.
In most cases, I use a hunch,
or solid information based on facts.

But maybe this dream is trying to say
something that might save me embarrassment or
    pain.
If our dreams can truly provide us with some kind of
    guidance,
then I guess I can't complain about the message it
    provides.

47

SOMETHING FROM A DREAM

This thing that someone just said
made me stop and stand up straight.
I looked around in surprise and wariness,
wondering if the situation was about to escalate.

Another person said the exact same thing
they had said in a recent dream.
Now that they have said it in real life,
I can't help but wonder what it means.

These incidents have happened before, in a different
    way.
I once saw something that I had first seen in a dream.
Then there was when I saw someone from a dream in
    real life.
It makes me wonder if these things are more than
    what they seem.

Usually, nothing major ever happens in the end.
It's a curious and puzzling thing to go through.
I'm usually more cautious and wary when it happens
and wonder if there's something that I must say or do.

65

48

A STORY DREAM

A man stalks a woman who has the same name
and looks exactly like his dead wife.
I wake up from that dream and turn it into a novel,
using similar elements from my own life.

Or a dream unfolds that my dream man is in,
but unlike the others, it is an entire tale.
I wake up and write the story that I just dreamed,
using research and my imagination to add detail.

Sometimes I'm inspired to create something new
or get a solution when all I can draw is a blank.
I get ideas for things to try or new places to explore.
For all this, I have my dreams to thank.

Dreams can be so creative and exciting
and inspire us with ideas to think about.
They have a way of helping us see in a new light
and use our own creativity to figure things out.

49
ONCE UPON A DREAM

We met once,
in a dream.
It was just us two.
Strangers then,
we both had feelings
and these feelings were so true.

We met again
in many dreams that followed
and our love stayed strong.
Nothing could separate us;
we enjoyed each other's company.
Being together was never wrong.

We meet still
only in my dreams,
even after all these years.
If only we were physically together to share our love
in a world that doesn't require me to sleep to get
    there,
but we are not, and it fills my heart with tears.

About the Author

Dawn Colclasure is a Deaf burn survivor whose incredible journey from surviving abuse to embracing a fulfilling life serves as an inspiration to all. She resides in Oregon with her loving husband and children. Dawn's evocative articles, essays, poignant poems, and captivating short stories have graced the pages of both regional and national newspapers, prestigious anthologies, acclaimed magazines, and reputable E-zines. With a background as a former journalist and poetry editor, she has channeled her creativity into over four dozen books, including "365 TIPS FOR WRITERS: Inspiration, Writing Prompts, and Beat The Block Tips to Turbo Charge Your Creativity," "Parenting Pauses: Life as a Deaf Parent," "On the Wings of Pink Angels: Triumph, Struggle, and Courage Against Breast Cancer," "A Ghost on Every Corner," and her deeply personal autobiographical poetry collection, "Touched by Fire."

Dawn is not just a prolific writer but also a dedicated publisher of the free monthly newsletter, The SPARREW Newsletter, and a respected monthly columnist for First Chapter Plus Magazine. To connect with her and explore her literary world, visit her websites at https://dawnsbooks.com/ and https://www.dmcwriter.com/. You can also follow her on Twitter at @dawncolclasure and @dawnwilson325, where she continues to inspire and uplift with her words.